This Is an Ocean

Gina Zorzi & Joi Washington

This is an ocean.

Oceans have water.

This is salt.

Ocean water has salt in it.

Some oceans look like this.

Some oceans look like this.

7

Surface

surface
under water
ocean floor

There is lots of sun here.

8

Seagull

There are birds.

Seaweed

There are plants.

10

Striped Mackerel

There are fish here, too.

Underwater

surface
under water
ocean floor

There is some sun here.

Black Spotted Sweetlips Fish

There are lots of fish.

13

Hawksbill Turtle

There are turtles.

Bottlenose Dolphin

There are dolphins.

15

Humpback Whale and Calf

There are whales.

Lemon Shark

There are sharks, too.

17

Camouflage

Mackerel

Barracudas

Manta Ray

Whale Shark

All of these animals look like the water.

Tiger Shark

Look up, they look white.
They look white like the water above.

19

Blacktip Reef Shark

Look down, they look black.
They look black like the water below.

Ocean Floor

There is a little sun here.

21

Lion Fish

Porcelain Crab

There are fish and crabs.

Sea Grass

Rocks

There are plants and rocks.

23

Camouflage

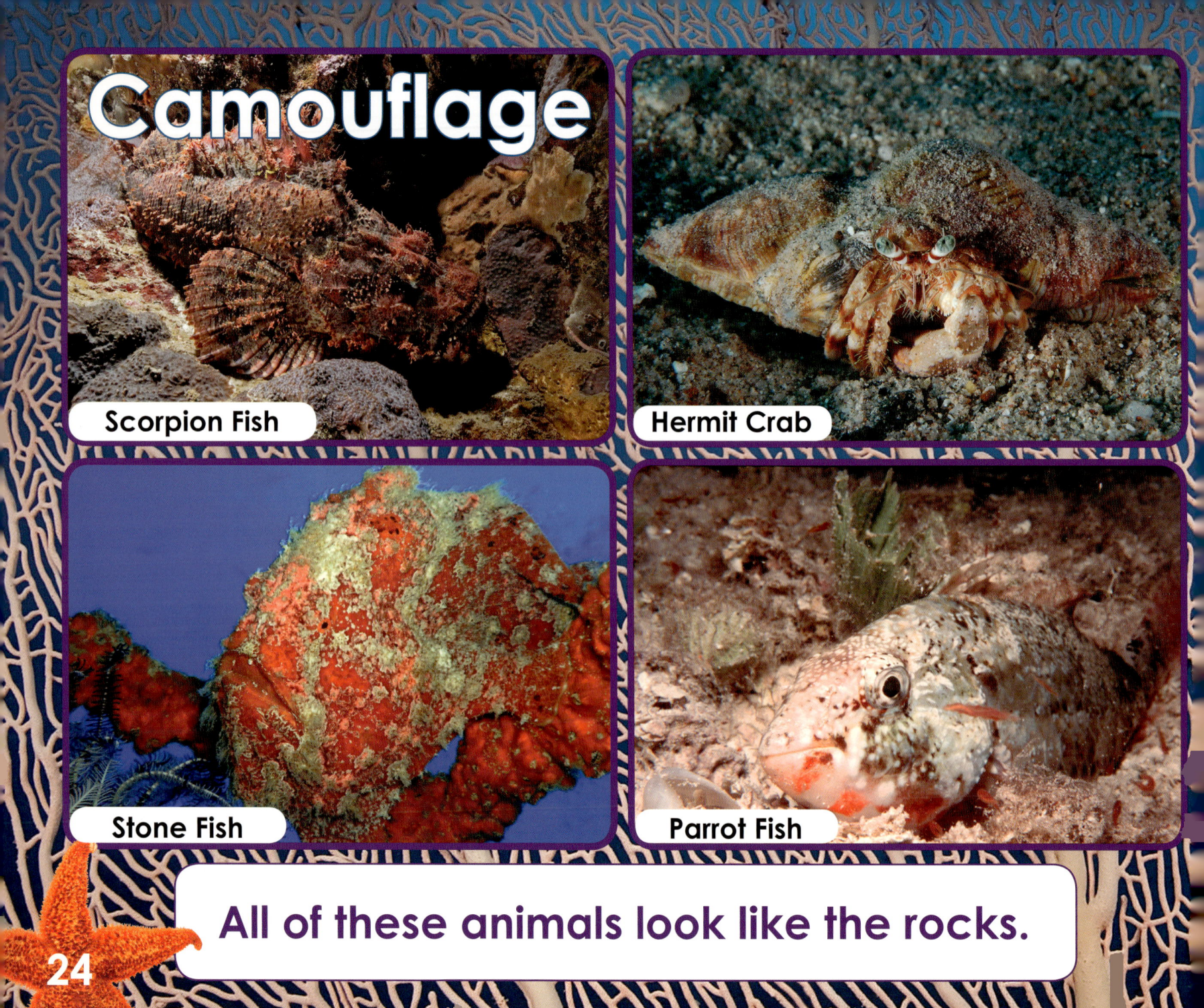

Scorpion Fish

Hermit Crab

Stone Fish

Parrot Fish

All of these animals look like the rocks.

Octopus

Can you see the octopus?

25

An Ocean Food Web

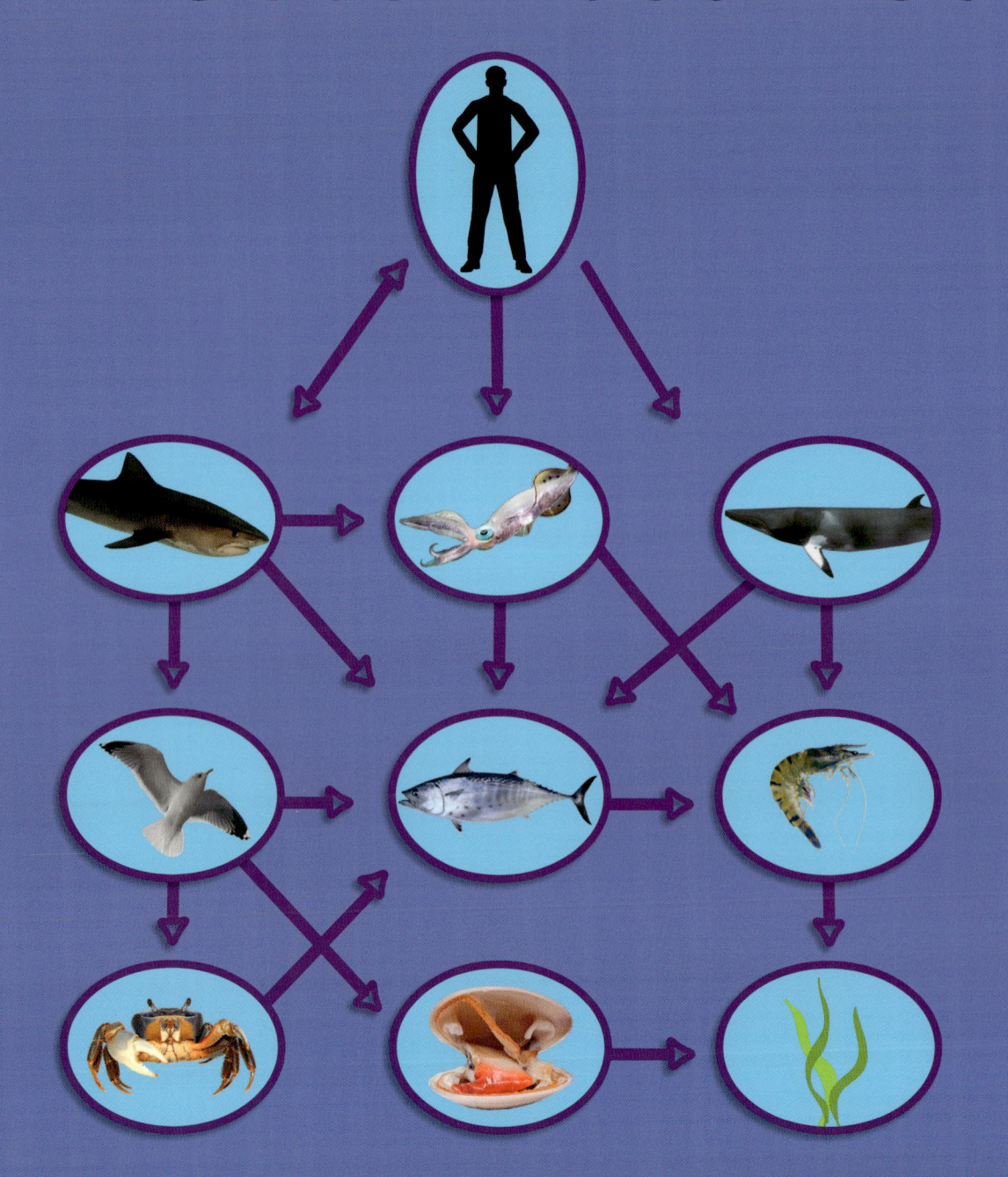